THE BEST OF
YANNI

Transcriptions and Arrangements by
RICHARD BOUKAS

"Music is like creating an emotional painting.
The sounds are the colors."

...Yanni

ISBN 0-7935-1709-5

HAL•LEONARD™
CORPORATION
7777 W. BLUEMOUND RD. P.O. BOX 13819 MILWAUKEE, WI 53213

FOREWORD

This collection of compositions was compiled to answer the requests of many of my fans that the music, which they've come to know through my concerts and albums, be made available in written form.

It is rewarding to me that so many people are inspired by the music I create, and it is with my deepest gratitude to them that I share this collection with you.

Through my music, I try as honestly as I know how to communicate emotion and experience. I hope that my creations will help people in their lives and make them feel better about themselves and the world in general. As an eternal optimist, I continually strive to create hope and optimism for the future in my music.

Creativity is an inherent human quality of the highest order. When we create, we become more than the sum of our parts, and I believe we all possess this ability.

My hope is that, as you play this music, you will experience your own creativity, and discover the unique paintings of life which only you can express.

Yanni

THE BEST OF
YANNI

CONTENTS

BIOGRAPHY

Yanni, the internationally acclaimed composer, performer and recording artist possesses the rare musical gift of clearly expressing emotions. Much like the great classical composers of the past, his music creates a profound impact on the listener which transcends mere entertainment.

Through sold-out tours, rave reviews, performances with major symphony orchestras, constant television exposure and the sale of millions of albums, Yanni has succeeded in presenting something new to contemporary audiences – music that celebrates the potential of the individual. His powerful and uplifting orchestrations are at once classical and contemporary, and represent thoughtful insights into the human condition.

Born in Kalamata, Greece to a family with music in its soul, Yanni's natural music gifts, such as "perfect pitch", and his composing skills were apparent at an early age. Self taught as a youngster, he developed an impressive proficiency at playing the piano. Yanni's multi-faceted talents were not limited to music alone. When he was 14 years old, he broke the Greek national freestyle swimming record.

After graduating from high school, he traveled to the U. S. to attend the University of Minnesota where he received his Bachelor's degree in psychology three years later.

By this time, music had begun to take over his life. He gave up pursuit of a Ph.D. in clinical psychology to dedicate himself to working on his music full time.

Yanni's natural inclination to experiment has broadened his musical horizons throughout the course of his career. A very focused individual, he spent 15 hours a day at the keyboards, worked as a studio musician, toured extensively with the popular cult rock band, Chameleon, and established himself as a performer, writer and producer. Over time, the combination of natural talent, hard work, experimentation and creative genius evolved into a distinctive musical style and expression.

Soon after the release of his first album, Yanni joined the top selling recording artists in the genre of contemporary instrumental music.

Beyond his recording career, his compositions have been used extensively by television networks for a variety of movies, news and feature productions including the Olympics. In addition, Yanni has established a successful film scoring career with soundtracks for movies, documentary films and network commercials.

In concert, he also attracts a very diverse following. His music has become a common ground where generations meet. From teens to the elderly, his fans represent a virtual melting pot of age groups and walks of life, and are testimony to the universal acceptance of the music created by this international musician for all seasons.

"I have a lot of hope for modern instrumental music," says Yanni.

And modern instrumental music looks to Yanni for hope.

ALMOST A WHISPER

Composed by YANNI

D.S. al Coda

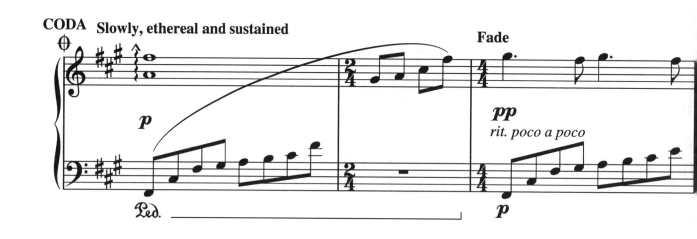

CODA Slowly, ethereal and sustained

Fade

FIRST TOUCH

Composed by YANNI

With Graceful Movement (= 108)
Full, rich tone

With pedal on down beats

Delicately, ringing

8va- - - - - - - - - -

loco

With clarity, as in opening

mp

MARCHING SEASON

Composed by YANNI

With more determination

Lightly, with some sense of resolution
(2+2+2+3)

THE MERMAID

Composed by YANN

CODA

Pointed, with a Greek folk-dance flair

With a marked vigor

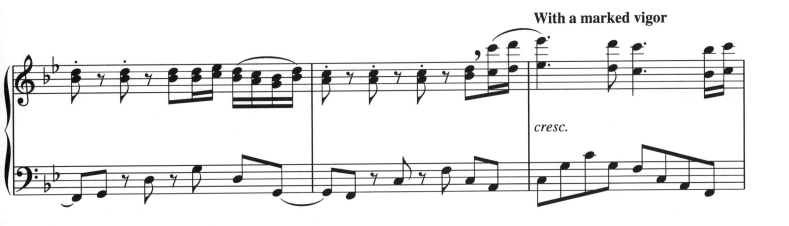

cresc.

SECRET VOWS

Composed by YANNI

To Coda ⊕

Sweeping, rhapsodic

D.S. al Coda

CODA

decresc. poco a poco

$\boldsymbol{p}$ molto rit.

Ped.

Ped.

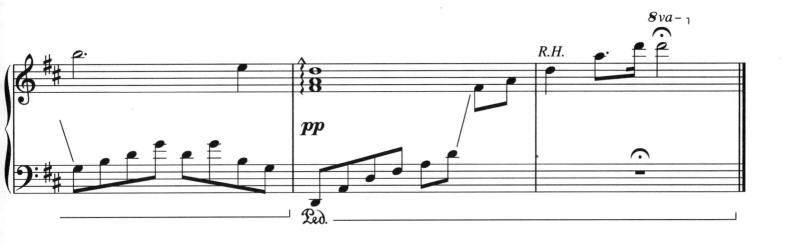

$\boldsymbol{pp}$

R.H.

8va-

Ped.

NOSTALGIA

Composed by YANN[I]

*Applies to R.H. only when indicated.

In "two", with sense of anticipation (♩♪ = 80)

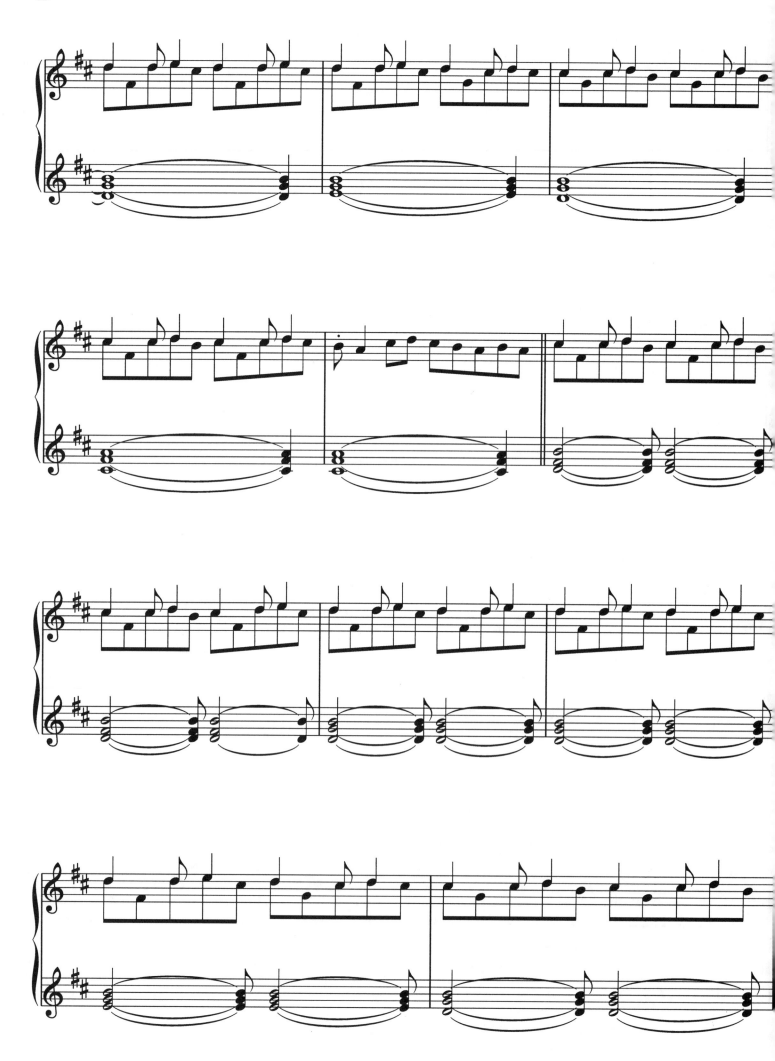

THE RAIN MUST FALL

Composed by YANN

Driving Half-time Feel, with strong backbeat ($\quad$ = 138)

Solo section:
Play as written, then solo R.H. ad lib.
Build with each 8-bar phrase.

REFLECTIONS OF PASSION

Composed by YANN

Gentle Waltz tempo ($\quad$ = 138)

rit.

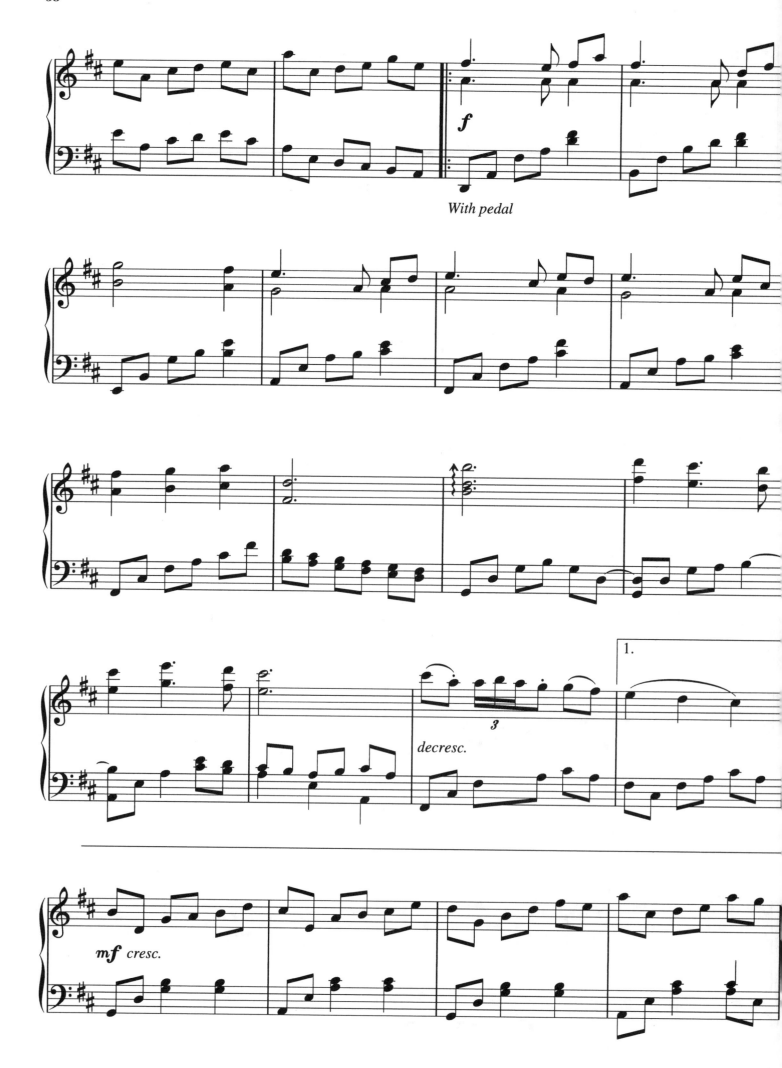

With pedal

(8-bar chord pattern) (Continue on cue after solo)

* These are pitch wheel bends on a synthesizer. Execute them as such, as equipment allows.

SWEPT AWAY

Composed by YANNI

TRUE NATURE

Composed by YANNI

Proudly, open sounding

To Coda I
To Coda II

A WORD IN PRIVATE

Composed by YANNI

Relaxed but majestic (♩ = 84)

Innocent, slightly halting

With pedal

Y A N N I DISCOGRAPHY

Keys To Imagination ....Private Music, 1986

Out Of Silence.............................Private Music, 1987

Chameleon Days..........................Private Music, 1988

Optimystique (reissue).................Private Music, 1989

Niki Nana ....Private Music, 1989

Reflections Of Passion ....Private Music, 1990

In Celebration Of Life ....Private Music, 1991

Dare To Dream............................Private Music, 1992

Richard Boukas is a recognized New York recording artist, composer, author and educator.
He currently tours with his Brazilian Jazz ensemble, AMAZONA, whose CD for Jazz Essence is his third release.
In 1989, Richard prepared orchestral transcriptions of Yanni's music for concerts with the Dallas Symphony Orchestra.